ECONOMIC ALPHABET

an irreverent guide to finance for the layman

by

Michael Becket

A Money-Go-Round guide from The Daily Telegraph

flame books

First published in book form by Flame Books 1976

ISBN 0 905340 00 0

Printed in Great Britain by
Cox & Wyman Ltd, London, Reading and Fakenham

Introduction

In the last twenty years pay has risen dramatically, people have felt more secure in their jobs and many have joined the affluent society. The vertical inflation of the seventies, taxation's steep inroads into income and the recent rise in unemployment have not changed the picture much, though for a time at least many of us are having to scale down our expectations about our material future.

Higher incomes have led to increased saving, if only because the inherited caution of not immediately spending everything we earn is not easily thrown to the winds, even when inflation threatened to make a pound saved worth nothing in little more than three years. Perhaps especially not then.

Savings are part of my job and the work of my colleagues in the City Office of The Daily Telegraph. Since Harold Macmillan said "You've never had it so good" in July 1957 (a slogan first coined in the American presidential election of 1952) interest in saving in all its forms has grown at an accelerating rate. Buying houses with a mortgage loan, insuring one's life, buying savings certificates or shares on the Stock Exchange are different ways of saving – and there are many more.

The sock and the mattress no doubt still take deposits but anything more sophisticated tends to baffle, even worry, those who save. What is encouraging, particularly to us, is that they are keen and determined to know more.

Throughout the week, but particularly in Family Money-Go-Round on Saturday, we in The Daily Telegraph endeavour not only to give sound guidance about all aspects of personal saving, but also to offer some instruction in the basics of economics, finance, saving and investment. In ten years as City Editor, I cannot believe there is a subject within our sphere, from backwardation to inflation accounting, which we have not tried to explain at least once. Our explanations will continue.

Meanwhile it seemed a good idea to put between stiffer covers some of the material that does not date. Hence this book, the first of its kind. It defines most of the words and terms that make up the short-hand of finance, in a manner that neither terrifies nor distorts.

When, as week after week they do, readers write to ask for notes or articles telling them in words they understand about the dollar premium or contangos or the International Monetary Fund or any of the other mysteries, I shall, with a clear conscience, refer them to this brief and readable book.

Kenneth Fleet
City Editor
The Daily Telegraph

Account

Being the eccentric British place it is, the Stock Exchange breaks up its calendar in a different way from everyone else – not into months or weeks but into accounts which are usually a fortnight long but stretch to three weeks over Bank Holidays.

An account is also a broker's bill, and the day it is presented is the account day (presumed to be paid immediately since it is also called settlement day). This is 11 days after the end of the account in which the deal took place.

Shares bought and sold within the period of one account do not pay stamp duty and pay less broker's expenses through attracting only a single commission. So if you know your broker and the market you can buy and sell and collect your profit, without putting down a single penny.

Arbitrage

Though the world of money is a more responsive market than most (the Stock Exchange is frequently – but wrongly – cited as a rare example of the economist's perfect market), there are still lags between one part of the world and another, and sometimes between one side of town and the other.

So if the dollar were cheaper in Zurich than London it might be worth buying them there, selling in London and reconverting to Swiss francs. You would then end up with more cash than you started with (though you would have to deduct the costs). Similarly if the price of a share varied from centre to centre it might pay an international operator to, say, buy in London and sell in New York and pocket the margin. This benefiting from differential rates is arbitrage.

The same process can also apply to all sorts of commodities, the most common one recently being money, as interest rates have fluctuated too fast and too irregularly. At one time overdrafts were cheaper than the commercial money market and shrewd companies quickly drew as much out of the bank as their manager would let them get away with, and put it out into the market.

Asset Value

There are a number of ways of working out the assets of a

company, and they reveal a lot about it as an investment prospect: how much shareholders get if it goes bust, how tightly its finances are administered, and so on.

For instance, if a company went under and its assets were sold off and distributed among creditors, the amount left over after paying liabilities and preference holders is called its net equity assets – this is what ordinary shareholders could get. In practice there is often nothing left.

Accounting peculiarities ensure the figure is not that easy to arrive at – in any case there are problems with goodwill, stocks, and work in progress.

There are other useful pointers. If the net asset value per share (surplus of assets over liabilities, divided by the number of shares) is much higher than the share price, the company often presents an open invitation to a takeover bid as the buyer would be picking up the assets on the cheap.

Even if the value is lower than the share price, it may be misleading if it includes freehold land which has not been revalued recently.

Then there is the net current asset value, and this tells you something about financial control of the company. This figure is calculated by taking short term assets (cash in bank, debtors, stocks, work in progress) and deducting current liabilities (creditors, overdraft, other short term borrowings).

The final figure in a modern company should be negative, and the final debit should roughly equal one year's pre-tax profits. Anything much greater shows weak financial control and a company likely to be strapped for cash, much less and it is undergeared.

Averaging

If you own shares and the price falls, you can buy some more at the lower price and so reduce the average cost of your holdings. This is called pound cost averaging. The same obviously applies on a rising price.

It can be a dangerous practice if the small investor indulges in it just to affect the average cost, because each share purchase should really be a rational decision in its own right.

Backwardation

One term with two meanings is peculiarly confusing. One meaning of backwardation is a discrepancy in the price quoted by two jobbers so great that there is obviously some mistake somewhere.

Another, more common, meaning is the payment (quoted as so much per share, say 2p) by the seller of shares to compensate the buyer for allowing a later delivery and so foregoing his rights to delivery of the shares when the rules say he could get them.

Balance of Payments

A popular but crude and unreliable indicator of the success of a nation's overseas trade. Since it is often taken as the gauge of the country's financial health, watching it becomes an addiction, but it can be a debilitating habit. *Warning*: watching the United Kingdom's balance of payments can damage your health.

In fact the final figure is the comparatively small difference of two very large figures (imports and exports) and also includes monumental cash flows which can render the final figure all but meaningless.

For instance, if United Kingdom interest rates are high foreigners bring their money here to earn lots of British money (but high interest rates may make it impossibly expensive for United Kingdom companies to invest), and this helps the balance because it shows as a cash inflow. (Obviously the rates cannot indefinitely be kept high since if nobody wants to borrow, the rates must fall.)

Another apparently healthy effect is produced by large companies and nationalized industries borrowing money overseas to spend in Britain.

The balance of trade does separate the figures by omitting capital flows and shows more clearly whether a country is paying its way with its exports. Even then the sum has nothing necessarily to do with the state of the country's economy which could stagnate though exports boom. In Britain's case one should also separate visible and invisible trade since although visibles have rarely shown a surplus, the invisibles (shipping, insurance, banking, dividends, tourism, etc.), have helped to offset the deficit.

A deficit is not necessarily the symptom of disaster some politicians (e.g. Mr Harold Wilson in the past) have claimed. Obviously not every country can run a surplus, by definition – one man's debt is another man's credit – and for instance the United States outflow of dollars fuelled the growth of world trade. But if a country persistently ran large and growing deficits other countries would in effect be subsidising its economy and would get disgruntled. One way their concern would show is by loss of faith in the country's currency.

Bank for International Settlements

Originally set up to administer debt payments among European countries in the 1920s. The aim of the Bank for International Settlements has been to confine discussions to finance and exclude politics. As its original function declined BIS has become a talking shop where European central bankers discuss at their monthly Basel meetings the problems of the international monetary system, but it still does a little Eurodollar business on behalf of the central bankers, implementing their collective decision.

Base Rate

Heavily overdrawn bank customers forced to pay more than base rate for their cash may think it well named. It is the rate of interest set by the banks – in effect the four big clearers (Barclays, Natwest, Midland and Lloyds) – on which they base the rates for loans and deposits. The level is set at whatever the banks think they can get away with.

The market was supposed to be freed but in such an oligopoly there is precious little competition in rates: none of the big four gets out of line for more than three weeks.

Now the base rate is loosely connected to the prevailing money market rates and companies attempting a spot of arbitrage are firmly discouraged by the banks.

But you do not pay base rate for your overdraft, oh, dearie me no. Local authorities and nationalised industries would pay ½ p.c. over, blue chip companies (like ICI, 'Shell', Beecham) would pay 1 p.c. over, and the impoverished private customer pays 3 p.c. to 5 p.c. over, depending on his luck and the toughness of his bargaining.

And if you put your wealth into the bank as seven-day money you would generally get 1½ p.c. under base rate. Money on three-month call is more closely related to the money market.

Bill Broker

In theory somebody who trades in bills of exchange (qv) who could be acting either on his own account or merely as an intermediary; in practice the term is used synonymously with discount houses (qv) who in fact act as principals.

Billions

There was a time when we talked with awe of thousands of dollars, much less pounds, and a millionaire was rich. It is a sign of the inflationary times that billions creep increasingly into conversation. The trouble is that there is no standard billion. The Americans, who already have a smaller gallon (we have the imperial gallon, which even sounds bigger), have a smaller billion as well. A thousand million is an American billion while in Britain a billion is a million million.

But to add confusion to a simple national difference, a few United Kingdom magazines, presumably hoping for American circulation, have without explanation started using the slim foreign billion. So if you suddenly see a headline which says Britain's deficit is £2 billion, don't panic, the journalist has just used the wrong expression. If that still confuses you, think of India, where they have a lakh, which is 100,000, and Americans talk about trillions (which is just a British billion), and zillions and the Continentals talk of milliards, which are just American billions. That sounds like schoolboy language. Perhaps it would be safest to go for the undisputed scientific notation of 10 raised to the requisite power.

BILLIONS

Bill of Exchange

A written undertaking to pay a specific sum of money – e.g., a cheque – usually post-dated. The recipient can endorse the paper and pass it on for his own payments virtually as cash – so long of course as the original signer (called an acceptor because he accepted liability) is a sound man. Since payment on the bills is some time hence, if the owner needs cash before maturity he can also sell them to a discount house (qv) which obviously charges for foregoing immediate payment. Banks sometimes also discount trade bills.

Blue Chips

This is an American term which has now become fairly generally accepted in Britain. It is used to describe the best and safest sort of enquity, usually of sizeable companies. The expression comes from gambling where the highest value betting chips used to be coloured blue.

Bonus Issues

A parcel of free shares kindly dropped into the unsuspecting investor's lap through the kindhearted generosity of the company in which he owns shares, is called a bonus issue – see also Scrip. For tax purposes the bonus issue shares are taken to have been acquired at the same time as the original holding and so are liable to the same tax.

Boom

A word which may be remembered by some of the older readers, it can also be associated with Concorde – but only by sound.

In this country it was usually applied to sharp bursts of over-rapid, unsustainable growth but in economics, during happier times, boom was the word used to denote expansion, increasing production, rising living standards, growing investment and falling unemployment.

If it ever recurred the ecologists would probably start scouring the gilt off the gingerbread by pointing to accelerating depletion of resources and the iniquity of growth in a world full of hunger. Is nothing free of guilt any more?

Bretton Woods

In July 1944, 44 nations got together in the small New Hampshire town of Bretton Woods to build a new post-war financial world. What they wanted was greater international stability, and part of the programme was to set up two new institutions, the World Bank (qv) which is a fund and the international Monetary Fund (qv) which is a bank.

The intention was to fix parities to prevent competitive devaluations and to promote world trade by giving businessmen greater assurance about the value of their foreign exchange earnings. To some extent and for a time it worked since international trade did flourish and currencies did become convertible. But the rigidities of the system caused its downfall.

Parities could not remain fixed for ever and the levels became points of such national pride that the distortions of delayed devaluations caused serious disturbances to national economies.

So the careful process of setting rates of exchange has long been submerged in a flood of floating currencies. And the huge outflow of United States dollars which at first helped to lubricate trade, eventually started worrying people to the point where their confidence in the dollar was undermined. Since the dollar was keystone of the graceful Bretton Woods arch, its removal caused the final collapse of the agreement.

In August 1971 President Nixon declared gold and the dollar were no longer interchangeable and with loud acclaim the agreement was buried, though the discrepancy between American gold reserves and the volume of dollars floating around had for a long time made convertibility a nostalgic fiction.

But the two institutions spawned by the historic conference are still with us and helping to iron out some world financial problems.

Brokers

Dealing on the Stock Exchange takes place between brokers and jobbers. Brokers come into contact with the public and make their money from dealing on behalf of investors and taking a commission for their trouble.

Being close to the market they are also presumed to be in the know and advise clients on how to spread their investments, and from time to time issue circulars on specific companies or industries to their more valued larger clients. These usually contain an elaborate breakdown of the figures available about an industry plus some forecasts.

Bulls and Bears

Among the Stock Exchange's curious bestiary (see also Stags, though prudence prevents discussing 'sharks') are the 18th-century inventions bulls and bears. Theories on the origins abound: the huntsman who sold the skin before the bear was killed (now called going 'short'); or from bare in being devoid of stock; or because bears knock victims down while bulls toss them up; or because John Bull was considered a portly optimist.

And so, still, a bull is an optimist and bull markets rise, and bears are gloomy and bear markets fall.

When jobbers are feeling bullish about a company they 'go long', but if they are bears they 'go short' and sell shares they do not own on the assumption that when the time comes for delivery they can buy them cheaper.

Capital/Current Account

The balance of payments is essentially composed of the difference between what we buy and sell abroad, and this shows just how effectively we are paying our way – or more often not paying our way. To paraphrase Mr Micawber: Exports £1,000 millions, imports £1,005 million – result misery.

That is the current account – it includes visible trade (imports and exports of goods) and invisible trade (income and payment for services and dividends). On top of that is the amount foreigners deposit in British banks, or cash used for investment.

That comes under the capital account. The part of that which is essentially on short-term loan and so can be quickly recalled, used to be called 'hot money' though it seems to have cooled off somewhat recently and does not flow round the world with the unsettling abandon of a few years ago.

More tepid still are the shares and property held by foreigners, and fairly cold is the industrial investment in plant and factories. The total will depend on the difference between the willingness of foreigners to invest in Britain and the eagerness of British companies to export their cash into foreign investment.

Capitalization Issue

Official description of a bonus or scrip issue (qv).

Certificate of Deposit

There are occasions, believe it or not, when large companies have surplus cash. If there is say £300,000 lying around idle because there are no immediate suitable investments for a year or so, the company puts it with the bank on deposit. Since the greater the stability of the money (the longer the deposit) the higher the rate of interest, the company undertakes to leave its cash there for a year. In return it gets a receipt – a certificate of deposit – stating the amount, interest, and length of time left there.

If circumstances suddenly change and the company decides it needs the money after all, it cannot withdraw it from the bank because it promised not to and the bank has therefore lent it on. So it sells the CD to a discount house (qv). The amount raised will depend on the prevailing rate.

What is a trifle perplexing at first is that the discount house gets the money for buying the CD from the banks in the first place. But in fact this is just another example of the cash swishing round fast enough to make sure none of it sits idle for a second – part of the City's pass the financial parcel. And everybody is happy – the company gets its money when needed, the bank has dependable cash, and the discount house makes a profit shifting the money around.

All this really started in 1966 with the setting up in London of dollar CDs, and two years later sterling was added. Now the banks even use the process among each other, issuing a CD to another bank against a longer term loan than is normally handled by the inter-bank market. And once again the bearer bond – which is what the CD amounts to – can be cashed with discount houses which are always ready to make a market and so as jobbers they also help to stabilize interest rates.

Charts

The City chartists have little in common with Cobden and Bright of the nineteenth century franchise movement. Chartism now is a forecasting method which was for a long time regarded as half-way between reading tea leaves and a pseudo-scientific leg pull.

The theory was originally evolved by Charles H. Dow of Dow Jones in the closing years of the last century when he noticed that the fluctuation of share price averages tended to throw up regular patterns, and from these he could make fair predictions about future price movements.

There are primary trends (general bull and bear markets which, overall, last several years), secondary reactions (important declines and rallies interrupting the broad primary trends and lasting up to three months), and tertiary movements (daily fluctuations). The actual interpretation of the graphs however is complex and littered with strange jargon.

There is the 'head and shoulders' graph patterns which

presage a bear market, and 'reversed head and shoulders' for a bull market, and so on. There are 'support areas', and 'resistance areas', and 'triangles', 'trend lines' and 'channels'. And that is just the start.

Though the study is more seriously regarded nowadays. it is by no means infallible and there is little evidence that chartists are better prophets than others though they can add an extra dimension to share analysis.

The most serious opponents to chartism in recent years have been the computer based mathematical models in American business schools. They suggest that share movements may be random in the way the results of coin tossing are random – in fact charting the fall of a coin produces very similar graphs to the stock market.

On present knowledge it is almost impossible to be sensibly dogmatic either way.

Comecon

The Russians are against the Common Market and suggested Britain withdraw at the referendum. But they have their own equivalent called Comecon though that is actually called merely a Council for Mutual Economic Assistance by the member countries.

The members of that are Bulgaria, Czechoslovakia, East Germany, Hungary, Mongolia, Poland, Rumania and the Soviet Union. Yugoslavia and Cuba are associate members. There have been few referenda on whether the countries would like to continue membership.

Confederation of British Industry

Formed in 1965 at government instigation from a merger of four management organizations. Membership covers some 11,500 of Britain's half a million or so companies, and about 220 employers or trade associations.

Constant Prices

Would that they were. The fact that government statistics are expressed in 'constant prices' does not actually mean Whitehall suddenly thinks it has permanently cured inflation or is trying to pretend it has – though recurrent excessive public expediture might make one wonder. It is actually just a way of trying to get at the real changes in production, consumer spending, or whatever by removing the inflationary element. So the figures are expressed in 1970 £s or 1965 £s throughout.

This obviously has its advantages in seeing reality (inflation accounting inside companies has similar aims) but was one of the factors which got government spending controls into trouble in 1971 to 1975 and percipitated the change to cash ceilings instead.

Contango

Say an investor has bought shares with the intention of dealing within the account (i.e. dealing within the two-week period and so paying lower commission and avoiding stamp duty), but discovers at the end of the account that he is showing a loss.

He is convinced, however, that his judgment was right, only his timing was slightly out, and if he could only hold on for another account he would show the expected profit. So his broker arranges a contango, that is, he carries the deal over into the next account, for an extra commission though normally he will only do so for stocks which are extensively traded.

Convertibility

The ability to change the currency of one country into that of another. The practice of permitting convertibility was adopted by the main developed countries in 1958 and in some form or another it has been continued since. But since it is subject to the country's legal limitations, and since there are investment premiums, some are more convertible than others.

The idea is to convert fully and freely at the prevailing rate for trade and other specific purposes, but Britain has an investment currency, the French, Italians and Belgians for a long time had separate currency for investment and for tourism.

Many of the poorer countries simply opt out of the problem by not allowing conversion for fear that their citizens might sell their cash for hard currencies which are in short supply and would thereby further weaken the currency.

Convertible

One of the many types of stocks issued by companies (see also debentures, loan stocks, preference, ordinary shares, scrip issue). They are in effect fixed interest securities which can be converted into the company's ordinary shares at a predetermined date, say, in 20 years' time. So they offer the security of fixed interest with the prospect of capital gains if the company continues to do well.

If the company's profits do not soar the convertibles can remain just fixed interest stocks.

Cost-of-Living Index

Like most averages which try to represent a whole population from a miscellany of disparate figures, the Index of Retail Prices as it is officially called, represents nobody. For a start anybody wondering whether to take out another mortgage to pay the latest rate demand (but deterred by mortgage rates on his house which have already sent him to the edge of penury), would be amused that housing represents only 12½ p.c. of the index since mortgages are not included.

And the other goods, too, are weighted by their importance to the mythical man in the street. So there is the standard food basket which is recalculated each year, plus clothes and shoes, transport, drink and tobacco, fuel and light, household goods and services.

Since this average is so unrepresentative it is more use as a general indicator of the moves in prices than as much of a guide on how much any particular individual is spending. The index is, despite all these shortcomings, possibly the best we have and at least is not rigged to keep apparent costs down and people happy, as is the practice in some countries.

Coupon

The rate of interest attached to a fixed interest security is

COST-OF-LIVING INDEX

called the coupon because a small certificate is at the bottom of a bond or share certificate which is detached and frequently used to get interests or dividend payments. So by extension the actual rate of interest is frequently referred to as the coupon.

Crawling Peg

One of the proposed solutions thought to be the answer to the system of fixed international currency parities which the Bretton Woods agreement (qv) bequeathed to the world.

The idea was put forward at a time when the existing parities seemed sacrosanct and any substantial alteration a defeat. So the crawling peg would make for small and frequent adjustments which would seem less disastrous and would upset the system less. And it would remove the strains that holding too long to an untenable parity entailed.

One claimed advantage was that it would prevent speculators jobbing against a currency, but since the shifts would be automatic they would also be predictable and the speculators' push against a currency would soon be rewarded. Altogether, the more anybody thought about it the less sense it made: if you are going to make constant adjustments why not just let the currency find its own level. And so floating was born.

Cycles

There is a tide in the affairs of men, and though the ebbs and flows are clearly visible on any graph paper nobody has yet managed to put a stop to the sharp fluctuations in the economy.

The curious fact is that though cycles are often regular and hence predictable, the industries concerned still manage to invest at the peak leaving them with surplus capacity at the trough, and fail to invest at the bottom thus leaving themselves short of capacity at the top. This last syndrome has in the past resulted in vast import bills for Britain as importers have rushed to fill the gap.

The trouble is that companies say they cannot afford to do otherwise – that cash is short in the lean years and the specific demand in the anticipated peak is not predictable.

Debenture

Public companies operate on borrowed money from a wide range of sources and their success comes from the ability to make the money bring in greater return than the cost of borrowing. Shares are the best known types of borrowing but companies sometimes borrow long term cash and certify the loan with a sort of IOU called a debenture, which is sometimes repayable (or redeemable at par) at a specified time.

The debenture is usually secured as a mortgage on the company's fixed assets and therefore comes ahead of ordinary shares for payment of interest. The market price, like that of preference shares, fluctuates with the prevailing interest rates to keep the actual yield in the line, the rate being usually slightly lower than on preference shares.

As debentures do not benefit from higher profits they do not appreciate with the company's fortunes and have little appeal for those interested in capital gains.

Deflation

When an economy overheats (presumably as a result of people with money running round in search of goods to buy) governments try to reduce the rate of inflation, and its attendant pressure on costs and manufacturers, by deflating the country's economy.

The usual cure is to reduce demand since with less demand but the same amount of goods prices should in theory come down – or at least stop rising.

The trouble is it does not always work since reduced demand can cause a recession but leave inflation rampant, especially if unions become more militant not less and if social security is lavish while unit costs are increased by short time working. There is also the monetarist argument. But demand deflation has been the staple of UK government policy for some years.

This is fine if the inflation was caused by excess demand in the first place, but a pretty nasty medicine for industry, especially if the underlying cause was elsewhere. Like for instance higher raw material costs or increased wages. Which is why industrialists started to make loud and unhappy noises at the constant government use of stop-go which merely damaged industry but did not in the medium term stop inflation.

In theory if a high rate of inflation is caused by wages rising faster than productivity, the answer is to initiate an incomes policy, and if the cause is soaring material costs a country could re-value its currency. Unfortunately for economists, causes are not always so neatly attributable, and cures not always acceptable for other reasons.

Depreciation

The steady shrinking of the pound in your pocket is called domestic depreciation – that is, it has a gradually falling purchasing power (break into a 5p piece and before you know where you are it is gone), it also applies internationally – the pound in foreigners' pockets.

Since the collapse of the system of stable world currencies set up at Bretton Woods (qv) floating has been introduced, so instead of infrequent large downward falls in sterling we have a constant creeping loss, and this has come to be called the trade weighted depreciation. That is a measure of its value against other currencies rated by their importance to the UK overseas trade. But see Devaluation for how it all works.

Devaluation

A reduction in the value of a nation's currency in terms of other currencies. Devaluations in the past, when they happened at longish intervals and by large amounts, were given as a percentage of how many fewer US dollars one could get for £1. For example the latest, in 1967, was 14.3 p.c.

But since the advent of floating currencies (qv), a constant change in value in response to the market, the fluctuation is given in terms of an average of currencies weighted by their trade importance to the UK.

Devaluations become necessary when the costs of one country are rising faster than those of the rest of the world and so its exports become uncompetitive. The strain is exacerbated by the so-called speculators who shift their money from one weak currency to another, just ahead of changes in parities.

By the pressure they exert through weakening one by selling, and strengthening the other by buying, they make their prophecy self-fulfilling.

Much of this currency trade is actually done by prudent companies trying hard not to be left holding the wrong sort of cash, or hedging their bets against their contracts. Anyway, with floating, the dam effect of infrequent large devaluations has been removed and speculation now needs a shrewd and agile mind.

The major problem of devaluations is that they do not deal with the cause of the problem, the lack of a country's competitiveness, only with its symptom. So the remedy can only be a temporary palliative, like giving aspirin to kill the pain instead of an antibiotic to get rid of the infection. (See also Crawling Peg and Floating Currency)

Discount

The confusing things about the jargon of the Stock Exchange is not only that they take everyday words and make them mean something different, but often they make them mean two different things. So shares are at a discount when the price is less than the value at which they were offered to the public.

As a verb the meaning is different. The market is said to discount a future event when the present value of the share already allows for it. So a high price may discount an anticipated profit rise, and a low price discounts the effect of a supplier's strike. As a result, when the developments are made public the share price will not change.

Discount Houses

The chaps in top hats wandering with apparent aimless elegance through the City are not subsidised exhibits laid on by the British Tourist Authority to reassure foreigners that there'll always be an England, nor synthetic figures dreamed up by cartoonists. They could well be representatives of discount houses and as such an important channel of funds from banks to government. The top hats are a tradition and a uniform, the work arcane but fundamental.

They shift short term cash around the City, mostly taking it from the banks to sop up surplus liquid funds, and so ensuring that no money stays idle long. They pay the banks a higher rate than the banks paid and then buy Treasury bills (qv), bills of exchange (qv), short dated government stocks, fixed interest bonds and certificates of deposit. These are often returned to the banks as security, and qualify for the 12½ p.c. reserve asset ratio demanded by the Bank of England.

They also deal generally in these securities and so push cash around between banks, financial institutions and the government. As must by now be obvious, these boys live on a narrow margin determined by how shrewdly they foresee the trends in interest rates and so how great a differential they screw out of the volatile borrowed cash and the assets they buy. The problems are only aggravated by the undertaking of the 11 members of the London Discount Market Association not only to tender for the Treasury bills, but also to underwrite their weekly issue.

Disinflation

Growing economic sophistication enables us to distinguish between deflation, disinflation, stagflation, reflation, inflation, and hyperinflation. But knowledge has not yet led to understanding the causes or cures.

The difference between deflation (qv) and disinflation is that the latter is the target the authorities set – reducing the rate of inflation – while deflation (in the sense of cutting demand) is one of the methods they use.

Other methods are also available but which one is best depends on the cause of the inflation. If inflation is being imported with higher raw material costs upvaluing the currency would help since it makes imports cheaper. But this can be done only with a strong currency and underused domestic manufacturing capacity, since cheapening imports will boost demand. This can be tricky – it is just as bad to fall flat on your back as to fall on your face.

Revaluation is however no solution for countries with currencies already under pressure, or with domestic inflation as well, which unhappily is often the case.

Other methods of disinflation include prices and incomes policy. But keeping down wages merely puts up a temporary dam so when the policy relaxes the economy is flooded with pent-up demands; and keeping down prices starves companies of the profits they need for further industrial investment.

Governments can keep down the cost of living by subsidies, but unfortunately even that money has to come from somewhere and the long term effects can be dire.

Dividend Cover

Dividend cover is the number of times that a company's available profits cover the money needed for the dividend. It gives an idea of how much spare cash flow the company has and therefore how safe the dividend is.

Dollar Premium

The government's concern at preserving the strength of sterling led to exchange control regulations to restrict the buying by UK residents of the shares of companies not registered in Britain. Because the securities must be bought with 'security dollars' (dollars from the sale of the shares by other UK residents) or the shares themselves must be purchased from British investors, demand outruns supply.

So to get into these shares the investor has to pay an extra, a premium. The dollar premium is the percentage by which the London stock exchange price is higher than the prevailing price of the shares in New York, Montreal or wherever.

It is not just shares but overseas property and the like which have also to be bought with the premium currency.

The seller should in theory get this premium back (assuming that the premium itself has remained the same) but the Treasury now takes its cut of 25 p.c.

Dumping

A highly emotional international subject this. In essence it is the practice of selling overseas at prices lower than in the home market; sometimes it is defined as selling abroad at less than the cost of production plus a reasonable profit and selling cost.

Countries often suspect each other of doing this, and that causes bitter accusations and wild recriminations – especially from afflicted trade associations – but dumping is very hard to prove. Many countries which have muttered about Japanese overseas selling tactics for instance have pointed to the flexible price lists and complex negotiations over each deal, which make it very hard to establish a genuine home selling price.

Some countries get round this difficulty of proof by analysing the nearest equivalent home producer's costs, and if the importer is inexplicably cheaper they assume dumping until proved otherwise. Britain requires more direct proof and so seldom takes anti-dumping protective action despite the heartbroken pleas by home producers.

The action permitted by international agreement is a duty to be paid on imports to cancel the price advantage and so prevent them damaging domestic manufacturers. It makes sense, since the overseas company, having bankrupted the native companies (assuming its own finances can stand a longer strain) then has a monopoly with corresponding freedom over price and supply.

Equities

There is such a range of names for the bits of paper companies issue that professionals sometimes have to stop and think which one they are talking about. Equity is a common synonym for ordinary shares which are what most ordinary investors buy.

Holding them makes you a member of the company as part owner, and gives you a vote which is most commonly exercised at the annual general meeting and all too often not used at all. For the most part, only large holdings have a sufficiently large voice to change company policy but there have been examples of shareholder revolts.

Dividends on these shares come from what is left over from the profits when everything else has been paid for, and so at times of stress distribution may stop. As a result the price fluctuates with the fortunes (or expected fortunes) of the company and gives opportunity for cashing in on capital growth.

Eurocurrency

Despite the name this is not the outcome of currency integration among Common Market members. Far from it. For one thing monetary union is a long way off in spite of hopeful statements to the contrary, for another, Eurocurrency is actually non-European money.

The first such money was the Eurodollar. These are American dollars piled up in Europe as a result of lending and spending from the United States. They were put to work and used by companies which needed dollars but could not get them from America after the clamp down on outflow from the United States to improve the balance of payments.

A major advantage Eurodollars have is that they are not subject to any control and are widely acceptable as cash by most countries which might turn their noses up at some currencies.

Exchange Control

Britain has chronic problems with its balance of payments and so tries to prevent additional difficulties by stopping

large outflows of capital. Payments by UK residents to non-residents are therefore regulated under the Exchange Control Act of 1947. This permits current payments (such as for imports) but restricts capital leaving the country (it used to be the sterling area when that was still going).
(See also Dollar Premium)

Expenses

It costs money to deal in stocks and shares. There is the broker's commission (usually 1½ p.c. of the value dealt in), stamp duty and company's registration fee (lots of companies do not charge though). All these have to be covered on the buying and selling of shares before you can say you have made a profit, and the jobber's turn (the difference between buying and selling price) must be taken into account as well.

Small investors should remember that there is a minimum broker commission, usually in the region of £7 and likely to rise again soon.

Fiscal Drag

Fiscal drag is a cunning way for the government to take more money away from us without our noticing.

The British tax system is what is rather misleadingly called 'progressive' which sounds like a term of kindly approval (assuming progress is a good thing). It is not. It means that the tax rates get progressively higher as a percentage with the higher levels of income.

As inflation depreciates currency, incomes also rise – in money terms if not in purchasing power – and that means the government is taking a steadily larger slice of the increased paper. As more of the income lies outside allowances and the like, and as a larger portion moves into ever higher tax brackets, the state starts to take an increasing portion of incomes.

It has all sorts of unexpected effects like reducing consumption at times of inflation, increasing income tax without the nasty publicity, soaking the rich (and the not so rich), and giving the state a growing portion of the nation's money. To be fair, the government should raise the break levels at which you move into a higher tax bracket to keep pace with inflation. Can you remember when that last happened?

Fiscal Policy

This is part of government policy which deals with the way governments spend and raise their money and the way they manipulate the level of demand in the country through those actions.

In other words it covers the all but impossible task of the government of paying for its expenditure, and the way it nudges the economy by raising taxes.

If the economy were deflating too fast (there was a time when that sort of thing happened), the government could act on the situation by increasing its spending but not covering the increase by more taxation. So in fact fiscal policy covers taxation, the national debt and Government borrowing: demand management by government spending and revenue raising.

It is usually contrasted with monetary policy (qv). It is the result the government borrowing requirement has on the growth of the money supply on interest rates and on inflation.

There was a time when there were Keynesians who said inflation is caused by excessive demand. Then there were monetarists who said inflation was caused by the growth of money supply, and now we have economists who generally acknowledge that the two are connected and both must be considered together.

Fiscal Year

If you want to send your tax inspector a new year card it should of course arrive on April 6, for with the contrary approach of government departments, the tax authorities resolutely refuse to recognize the calendar the rest of us use.

There was the Julian calendar which was all right but lost 11 minutes and 10 seconds a year so that Pope Gregory had to shift everything round a bit in 1582. Henry VIII with splendid insularity would have none of this newfangled Continental nonsense so it was not until 1752 that Britain adjusted by which time the loss was 11 days and September 3 became 14 (and so provoked riots). Incidentally the Russians did not get around to it until 1918 which is why their October revolution actually happened in November.

Accounting and tax years have followed Customs, Commerce and Navigation with usual quarter days being chosen for accounting years. In 1800 it was January 5, but in 1832 they plumped for Lady Day which was March 25 but once 1752's missing 11 days are added back you get to April 5. Yes, it does sound implausible, but there you are. The American fiscal year starts on July 1 – there is probably a story to that too

Floating Currency

After years spent fighting reality several governments realized that the current exchange rate of a currency had no hallowed priviledge and was not worth defending to the last drop of gold. But rather than guess at the rate the currency would be worth at a time of trauma and overseas upheavals,

FISCAL YEAR

they allowed it to find its own level by a sort of free market economy.

This meant abandoning the Smithsonian agreement (qv), as well as Bretton Woods (qv), but at least it removed the stigma of devaluation (qv). It took some time to realize that the stability of fixed rates of exchange was bought at a dear price of substantial sacrifices by a country whose currency was under pressure. The rate was supported by the central bank (e.g. the Bank of England) buying its own currency and thus pouring out the hard-won foreign currency. And the government felt the best defence was a short term improvement in the balance of payments which usually meant stopping the economy dead as a way of reducing imports.

First major currency to take the plunge was Canada in 1950 whose temporary float lasted more than ten years. But over the past two or three years several countries have let supply and demand set the ratc. Thc stated intention is still to fix the parity once the currency has found its level at a time of stability. As a result some countries have indulged in the 'dirty float' – that is, pushing the currency to the level its ministers would like by quiet intervention in the currency market.

One drawback to the float is that it can sometimes lose the advantages of a devaluation. When a currency has been devalued balance of payments at first get worse as imports cost more but as they become exports things are better than before. But with a float it could happen that as things get worse the currency drifts again and so the country is permanently stuck in the darkest hour waiting for a dawn that never comes.

FOB/CIF

United Kingdom exports are normally counted FOB which is merely an old commercial abbreviation for free on board – i.e. the price covers the goods and getting them as far as the hold of the ship. The other way of calculating such values is CIF which covers cost insurance and freight – in other words the price covers the seller paying for the insurance and transport.

Until a few years ago exports were counted FOB and imports CIF which had some sort of logic since it dealt with the cost of goods at the point they crossed the coast, but the figures got a trifle confusing. So now Government statisticians talk about FOB values and separate the rest of the cost out into the so-called invisibles sector.

Forward Market

Dealings in commodities, currencies or securities for future delivery at rates which are fixed at the time the deal is struck are called the forward market to differentiate the deals from the spot market which is for immediate (or pretty quick) delivery. Obviously the juggling of forward and spot rates and transactions can be used not only for crafty speculation, but also as a safety net for users of the cash or commodity.

So a company which makes chocolate for instance might try to limit its potential costs by balancing the deals though roughly arranging purchases to cover prospective needs. In theory anyway.

This is also called by the intriguing science fiction title of futures market.

FT Index

It would be misleading to judge the trend of share price movements by just adding all the individual price changes. Some companies have a particularly volatile market because most of the shares are locked up and so a few transactions can cause sharp fluctuations. Also small companies frequently provoke speculative buying and cheap shares are more liable to large percentage swings.

So some indexes have been evolved to try and iron out these problems. The most commonly used is the *Financial Times* Ordinary Share Index usually just referred to as the FT Index. This consists of 30 selected shares, all active stocks of Britain's major enterprises and though the index has been going since 1935, the component companies do change. Rolls-Royce for instance was displaced even before it went broke by Allied Suppliers which was taken over and supplanted by Cavenham.

There is also an FT-Actuaries All Share Index which covers 500 industrial shares and though it tends to move with the Ordinary Index, it gets used much less.

Futures Market

See Forward Market.

GATT

Leading nations have realized increasingly that fighting each other with tariffs and trade restrictions in the long term helps nobody – it just slows down the flow of international trade which harms every country. So in 1947 they got together to set the rules for the laudable aim of liberalizing world trade.

The idea is that nobody is allowed to increase tariffs and General Agreement on Tariffs and Trade encourages people to lower them by multilateral agreements, and the Kennedy Round of tariff reductions was an example of this endeavour actually netting results. On top of that GATT outlaws favouritism and discrimination among the member countries.

In theory therefore a country cannot just slap on a massive duty to keep out competitors though there are escape clauses for countries getting into dire emergencies. When Britain for instance imposed an import surcharge other GATT members protested but did not act realizing the trouble Britain was in. In fact if the countries get irritated they can in theory retaliate against a miscreant by slapping on their own tariffs.

Unhappily the liberalization, which was GATT's original aim, is taking longer than hoped. Part of the reason is that free trade helps the strongest, most industrialized, and technologically most advanced countries. They are not the ones that need help and understandably enough the poorer countries are reluctant to forego the advantages of restriction.

Food is not covered, and neither are quotas which can be a very effective way of limiting imports of sensitive items.

Gearing

The ratio of company's borrowings from banks as overdrafts and in the form of debentures and preference shares, to ordinary shares (equity) is called its gearing. If there is a high proportion of prior charges before ordinary shares reach the head of the queue, the company is said to be highly geared.

The reason this ratio is of interest to the investor is that as the interest on the loans is fixed and obligatory, the ordinary shareholder's share drops very rapidly at times of low profits. When times are good however the amount available for equity distribution jumps sharply.

Frequently though it is cheaper for a company to raise an overdraft than issue shares so good management will maintain a balance.

Gilt-Edged

Now the term is usually applied to British Government securities which are reckoned to be as safe as you can get or, by extension, securities of the Canadian or Australian Governments, etc.

These fixed interest stocks guaranteed by the government are redeemed (bought back) between specified dates which can be up to 40 years away. Yield varies with price, which in turn is partly set by prevailing or expected interest rates – it is quoted as dividend yield (par value divided by price, times nominal interest), or redemption yield which includes the capital bonus when the government redeems at par – usually raising the cash by issuing more stock.

The amount on issue depends on government spending, borrowing, and monetary policy. Do not confuse with Treasury Bills (qv).

Gnomes

What ever happened to the gnomes of Zurich whose currency speculation was reckoned to undermine the currencies of honest hard working nations? For a start they have been going through a pretty rough time recently – the Union Bank of Switzerland alone dropped at least £20 million on currencies, and rumours since have put it at double that. Lloyds Bank in Lugano lost the bank £33 million on foreign exchange dealings.

During the oil price rise the gnomes lost a lot of money by selling sterling short, forgetting that the Arabs were putting their money into London – the Bank of England made about £100 million out of that miscalculation. Across the Continent banks have been buffeted by the problems: Herstatt and International Credit Bank failed, and others have been rocked by large losses.

In any case the disapproval has been falling away as hedging one's currency bets is seen as the most reasonable precaution companies can take to off-set potential threats to their trading profits. But not long ago it was the Swiss bankers who got all the stick for selling sterling and thereby weakening it to the point where devaluation was inevitable.

The naïvete of that political ruse is now clear – the attempt to blame rich and unnamed foreigners for a country's economic ills is an old trick which occasionally works.

People now understand that speculation against a currency is not always done from spite, nor is it always just a short cut to easy profits. It is merely the cautious placing of one's money where it will be safest. If sterling is being sold the reason is that the economy backing it is weak or ailing. Attacking the speculator is like blaming the thermometer because it is getting cold.

GNP & GDP

There is a surprisingly wide variety of ways for measuring the output of an economy and it can make a difference which one you use for the totals are seldom the same. First of all there is national product which includes all the country's production plus net property income from abroad. Leave out the property income and it becomes, reasonably enough, domestic product.

Both are usually referred to as gross (hence GDP, GNP) as if to make them sound bigger but in fact it just means depreciation has not been deducted. If it has, then the result is net.

The calculation for all this is usually at market prices but if you deduct indirect taxes such as VAT and add subsidies the result is at factor cost.

But that is not the end of the complications. Most of the items are included at price except public services (cost), the self-employed (imputed, which is the just statistical word for guessed), do it yourself, and housewives (ignored).

Since all the money made goes somewhere and is paid to

somebody, national product equals national expenditure. All nice and logical except that the results by the three methods – spending, income and output – never quite come to the same figure.

Gold

Although scornful of primitive tribes which use cowrie shells or cocoa as currency, we still rely as the foundation for our economies on a metal of little practical purpose save that it is inert and hence will not corrode. It is curious how gold has persisted as a store of value, continuing as mattress stuffing at times of uncertainty, to the exclusion of most other such goods.

It is still a main backing of national economies – reserves are in gold and foreign exchange. Fort Knox even had to have open day to show people that it was still filled with the ego-building yellow bars.

While people distrust paper money gold will continue to have its disproportionately great value since the desire to hoard it means it becomes the only currency with a steady real value in terms of goods. So far attempts to subvert its strength by creating 'paper gold' such as special drawing rights (qv) have not displaced the original, though at least the volume of world trade is not necessarily restricted to the volume of gold South Africa and Russia are prepared to release.

Between 1958 and 1970 the central banks tried to regulate the price of gold through the central pool to between $35 and $35.20, by buying when it fell below and selling when it rose above. Then, partly through South African dissatisfaction with this reduction of its potential foreign earnings prompting reduced sales, the price of gold so persistently tried to rise that the banks found themselves persistent sellers.

The choice was to give in and raise the price or to stop selling and ignore the free market. The banks opted to state their reserves at the $35 level to prevent the value fluctuating with world gold market, but freed the price which went on a long uptrend but since then fluctuated to its own level.

The French have been notorious gold hoarders for centuries (those mattresses must get frightfully lumpy) and now other countries are getting the habit. The South Africans are quickly taking advantage of the price rise by minting Krugerrands (made legal tender to avoid capital gains tax) and Britons have been flocking to buy the coins. With Americans being freed to buy gold the United States commodities exchange is dealing on gold futures.

This will of course divert savings from useful industrial investment to an unproductive Scrooge-like pile of coins. Perhaps the answer to that is to return to the renaissance habit of depositing the gold in a vault and using the receipts as currency.

The major trading nations would obviously like to get away from reliance on gold but it looks as if no other medium of exchange will command such widespread faith in our lifetime.

Green Pound

Yes, all pound notes are green because ... (insert your own racial prejudices) pick them before they are ripe. But Common Market pounds are greener than most. The EEC uses one of the innumerable definitions of its national common currency, the gold-related Unit of Account (qv), as the basis for pricing the common argicultural policy, and the conversion rate from this UA to sterling is the green £.

Valuation of this particular UA is not automatic though it is related to floating currencies, nor is it periodic, but is open to intergovernmental haggling. As a result, the green and normal foreign exchange pounds sometimes get out of line while the UK government is pondering where the balance of advantage lies.

The decision of when to change the parities and by how much is a trade-off between the interests of consumers who want a strong green pound to keep food prices low, and farmers who obviously want the exact opposite. Both this and the whole unit of account method seem to an outsider ramshackle and Heath Robinson, but the Common Market maintains it more or less works in practice.

Group of Ten

It is curious that the meeting grounds for economists, central bank governors, ministers of finance etc., continue to proliferate – there is the International Monetary Fund, the World Bank, the Group of Ten, the Group of Twenty, the General Agreement on Tariffs and Trade, the Organization for Economic Co-operation and Development, Bank for International Settlements.

The Group of Ten is a club of the finance ministers and top treasury officials from the ten rich non-communist countries who meet when the need arises. Since there is no staff, no fixed routines, the group tends to be more responsive to immediate problems than other organizations.

Another factor in favour of the Group is that it actually takes action such as organizing support for a country in need of help. Britain has been among the beneficiaries of this policy.

The members are the United States, Germany, France, Italy, Netherlands, Belgium, Sweden, Canada, Japan and Britain.

Growth Stock

Companies expected to do really well and make their shareholders a lot of money are called growth stocks. Usually the price is rather high and the yield pretty low because some of the growth is discounted but holders usually benefit as the share price continues to soar.

Hammered

When a broker goes bust he is not declared bankrupt but is hammered. The term arose from the traditional ceremony involved in declaring a member or firm a defaulter.

A waiter (an attendant – so called from the coffee house origins of the Stock Exchange) walks into the market, solemnly mounts a rostrum, hammers three times on the edge of it, and declares in ringing tones the name of the member or firm who has defaulted.

The Stock Exchange maintains a fund to protect its customers, the public, from losses as a consequence of a hammering. Fortunately it was not a common practice though the long 1973–75 share slumps caused an exceptional number.

Hedge

A vague and confusing term which just means taking prudent measures to protect yourself against the change in value of something. So investors can hedge against inflation by putting some money into equities as the prices are expected to rise in line with the falling value of money – all other things being equal.

Commodities markets show clearer examples, with dealings in futures being used to hedge against the current variations.

Hyperinflation

Everybody is agreed that this means fast inflation but not agreed on where the threshold is for hyper. Probably anything over 20 p.c. is a potential hyperinflation situation – i.e. an inflation that becomes so effectively self-feeding that it is no longer controllable by normal economic means.

At that stage money ceases to have any serious purpose as it can halve its value in a day and only constant overprinting with a new set of zeros keeps it in use at all. This happened in Germany in the 1920s and Hungary in 1947, when the billions and trillions became so meaningless that people reverted to barter, using cigarettes and chocolate as currency.

No economy can survive this unscathed: industry cannot

HYPER INFLATION

continue and savings cease to have any value. Disruption can reach proportions which affect the political stability of the country.

Inflation

As everybody must by now be only too aware, inflation means money loses its value. The causes and effects are subject of heated argument as much among economists as laymen.

Old style economics used to say that the two main causes were fast rising manufacturing costs working their way through to prices (so called cost push) – oil is an obvious current culprit as were for a time raw materials such as copper; and the other cause was demand outstripping supply which caused buyers to bid up the price of goods (so called demand pull).

A cause of recent inflation in Britain has been the rate of increase in wages. If pay goes up by more than production it is obvious that prices will have to rise and the workers will get larger amounts of money but it will not be worth more. The higher wage costs are passed on and everybody is back where they started – asking for more pay.

It is not a return to square one though if other countries contained inflation by improving productivity because in that case exports are lost, sterling is devalued and Britain is worse off than before. The ones who suffer in such circumstances are those on fixed incomes and with less negotiating power.

When wage restraint failed to stop inflation, since money supply, oil prices and raw material costs were major causes, the unions were moved to some specious arguments about incomes policy. But in fact it merely showed that effects seldom have a simple single cause.

A degree of inflation is accepted by most governments nowadays as harmless, perhaps even helpful in keeping the economy buoyant. When it becomes an accelerating spiral or when it endangers prosperity and the balance of trade, it is worrying. Nobody knows just when inflation starts to become self-generating. No country appears to have the solution, which must in any case vary with the balance of causes.

Inflation Accounting

Everybody now adjusts for inflation almost automatically: 'it only cost me £12, but that was four years ago, so heaven knows what it would cost now.' Yet company accounts have just been ignoring inflation, but it has failed to go away.

The accountancy bodies proposed a relatively simple method of adjusting every figure in a company's balance sheet by the retail price index, to give an indication of relative value since the index is a fair measure of the *current purchasing power* of the pound.

Some companies have protested that this CPP method is not quite a fair picture of what their assets are worth, since the cost of electronic microcircuits is not closely related to the cost of bread, and the price of factories and machine tools are different again. So they have suggested that physical assets be counted at *replacement cost.*

Their argument has been backed by the government appointed Sandilands Committee, which called its variant of replacement cost, *current cost accounting.*

There are arguments in favour of both, CPP is an independent adjustment while RC and CCA are subjective guesses; CPP portrays price but not value, while RC does not tell shareholders what their stake in the company is worth, and so on. Ideally there ought to be both, even if a caveat were added to explain that some figures were merely the directors' best estimate.

A problem is that since a number of companies are really making too little money at the moment to stay alive much longer, the inflation adjusted accounts would show them how dangerously they were living and force them to put up prices. And will the government accept the true (adjusted) figures for tax and price control?

The worry has been that if you institutionalize it, inflation is here to stay, but learning to live with it might at least deaden some of the pain – and reduce insolvencies. But once started the process is hard to stop and any number of figures could, might and should be index linked.

International Bank for Reconstruction and Development

See World Bank.

International Monetary Fund

The fund is one of the two enduring features of the ill-fated Bretton Woods agreement (qv), the other being the World Bank. It is in fact a bank to smooth out the fluctuations of the world trade cycle, preventing the catastrophic united plunge into depression which afflicted the major nations in the 1930s.

Each member country contributes a theoretical quota of gold and its own currency which the Fund lends to countries afflicted by short to medium term balance of payments difficulties. The idea is that if the problem is genuinely a transient one the country can with Fund help ease itself through it without the need for damaging deflationary cutbacks. But it is neither the Fund's job nor its intention to support ailing currencies against fundamental weaknesses.

When the loan comes to a country and the troubles are not self-evidently fleeting, the country has to reassure the Fund that the problem will in fact be made a short one by some sort of economic internal measures – these will also ensure that the country will be able to repay the loan in the three to five years the Fund likes.

As a result there was a tendency at one time in Britain to blame the IMF for the stop part of the stop-go cycle, since it asked for the indications of ability to pay which needed foreign exchange and hence a favourable balance of payments. But if a country is in the sort of chaos that it needs major loans to haul it clear, then it evidently needs to do something about its economy. To blame the IMF is merely to confuse the messenger with the message.

In any case the IMF is in no position to help everybody. The Fund is around $30,000 million but about a third of this is in minor countries' non-convertible currencies which nobody wants, and some is in gold which no country is likely to contribute while the valuation is still out of line with market rates.

Investment Trusts

Some companies deal in goods and some provide services. An investment trust is a company just like any other except that its sole purpose is to invest in other companies.

Its shares are quoted on the Stock Exchange and are traded in the normal way, with the price reflecting the astuteness of the managers. The charm of such outfits for the small investor is that they spread his cash, and hence his risks, among many companies and frequently many industries.

They are slightly different from unit trusts (qv) in being quoted, having a fixed number of shares, and a share price not being directly related to the price of the equities the trust holds. There are quite a number of them around, London and Edinburgh being the main centres from which they are run.

Invisibles

Not the world of leprechauns or delirium tremens – merely the international trade in services, as opposed to goods. This includes banking, insurance and shipping which are Britain's biggest invisible exports. Also lumped under this heading are dividends on overseas investments, the results of commodity and foreign exchange trading, air transport receipts and tourism.

There are also the profits from films and from plays which move to Broadway, royalties on books and records (the Beatles got their MBEs for that), and sales of patents and copyrights.

It is fortunate that Britain has a long tradition of shipping, a reputation for being an insurance centre, and has always had major investments overseas, either in foreign companies or in subsidiaries of UK concerns. It is the foreign exchange earnings from these sources of invisible exports that has helped to compensate for the tragic deficits on visible trade.

J Curve

When a country's currency is overvalued – a tricky mixture of trade and psychology – it eventually has to devalue. This used to by large intermittent downward leaps in the rate of exchange with gold and other currencies; nowadays more often by letting the currency find its own level vis-a-vis the others.

Either way the intention is to improve the balance of trade since devaluing the currency means that the country's exports will be cheaper in terms of other currencies which should therefore boost exports. Also imports should fall as they become more expensive.

And there is the crunch. Although this will obviously give a double boost to the balance of payments eventually through higher exports and lower imports, the initial effect will be negative. This is because the exports are made principally of imported raw materials and semi-finished goods which have become more expensive, so until the outward flow is really adding to the foreign exchange and the benefits become felt, the balance of payments dips.

Since there is (it is hoped) a short downturn, followed by a long upturn, the graph looks like a J leaning back slightly, Hence the name of the curve.

It is thought that floating currencies experience the danger that each time the poor figures at the bottom of the J emerge everybody abandons the currency yet again. And as the sleek rats are heading for the shore the currency dips again, and so hits another downward bit of a new J curve and so on. But growing international sophistication in floating currencies is perhaps reducing this danger.

Jobbers

These men are really the heart of the Stock Exchange – the men who actually make the market and deal with the stockbrokers who act for investors.

A jobber deals on his own behalf making often considerable profit from the difference between buying and selling prices. But of course as it is his own money he is playing with, a jobber carries considerable risk because shares he bought for his books yesterday may suddenly plummet leaving big losses on unwanted shares.

When an investor wants to buy shares his broker wanders round the Stock Exchange asking the prices from several jobbers. He will get two prices one at which the jobber will buy and a higher one at which he will sell – say 60p and 62p.

But sometimes the deal is open to haggling depending on the size of the block of shares (the jobber may not want too many of some companies) or the state of the market (he will be a bit wary at volatile times).

What happens is that the deal is closed at, say, 61½p. But the jobber may have been going 'short' – been expecting prices to fall and has none of the shares on his books. To find some he raises his prices to say 61p and 63p. If this succeeds and he manages to bring out a seller at 61p, his profit is the ½p difference, called his 'turn'.

The jobber's long term livelihood depends on his ability to anticipate the mood of the market and adjust his prices accordingly, and to widen or narrow his prices at times of 'one way' markets (only selling or only buying) to try to counteract the trend.

Kaffirs

Since the City and the Stock Exchange became more respectable, they have also become less whimsical. But shares which have been around for some time still retain their nicknames. Among these is Kaffirs for South African gold mining shares, Diggers for some Australian shares, and Gilts for government securities.

Individual companies are often referred to by abbreviated names such as Bats for British American Tobacco, Imps for Imperial Group, Tanks for Tanganyika Concessions and so on.

Keynes

John Maynard Keynes was that rare bird – an economist who proved he knew enough about how the system worked to amass a considerable amount of money, not only for himself but also for Kings College Cambridge. In addition to lecturing at Cambridge, he advised governments and after a spell in the Treasury during the First World War wrote The Economic Consequences of the Peace, which condemned the short-sighted policy pursued by the Versailles Treaty.

But the book which changed government attitudes to running their economies was the General Theory of Employment, Interest and Money which was published in 1936.

The basis of the theory was that laisser faire ought to be abandoned and the government ought to intervene to iron out the fluctuations of the capitalist system. At times of depression, Keynes pointed out, people spend less because they don't know where the next wage packet is coming from, and so aggravate the downturn by falling consumption. As more people are thrown out of work the cycle becomes self-perpetuating and can only be broken by an outsider.

The only outsider is the state, and Keynes said it ought to increase its spending to get more movement into the economy and so pull it out of the trough and reduce unemployment.

It is perhaps due to Keynes that the world has experienced no serious slumps since the publication of his book, but in

KAFFIRS

any case he certainly enlarged the scope of economic thinking, though inevitably the current crop of economists express doubts about some of his views.

Lame Ducks

The traditional expression for the hopeless and helpless, the phrase was appropriated by the last Conservative government to describe the failed sections of industry. The theory was that an industrial shake-out would topple over the lame ducks, and a good thing too since they were patently inefficient and unnecessary, and as such were diverting capital from more remunerative and necessary companies.

So as part of the philosophy of letting industry stand on its own feet, the lame ducks were to be allowed to stagger into an early grave. Then industry found itself standing not too squarely on its bleeding stumps, and as unemployment mounted, the government chickened out and started throwing money around like a drunken sailor (or a Labour government) in an effort to stem the politically suicidal rates of unemployment.

In terms of return on capital, Britain is knee deep in lame ducks. But the evidence is that in fact they are not draining much needed capital from the would-be successes. Companies have not been investing in more equipment because they do not see a continuing profit since they doubt the stability of the economy. But when social needs are seen to conflict with market economics it seems the short term social palliative always wins.

Loan Stock

This term is sometimes used as an alternative name for debentures and the two are similar in that both rank high for repayment, being classed as creditors, and interest is payable on both whether the company is earning profits or not. But debenture holders are usually secured creditors while loan stock is usually unsecured. These are among the many pieces of paper issued by corporations in exchange for a loan. (See also Equities and debentures.)

Mark

In the Stock Exchange a mark is not always the much-desired German currency, usually it is the actual price at which a deal is carried out. When dealers talk of marking down they do not mean that there is a steady decline in the price at which deals are concluded, but that jobbers are lowering their prices since they are doing no business. Sometimes it is done in anticipation of a lack of demand as when a company announces poor results. Marking up is the same thing in the opposite direction.

Minimum Lending Rate

The successor to bank rate in a free market. In the bad old days of officially imposed money rates, the Bank of England set the interest rate; now the free market demand for money sets the rate – unless the rate happens to be too low for the government's policy, in which case the Bank of England sets the interests rate.

If fact what happens is that the Treasury Bill (qv) rate, which really is determined by the prevailing conditions, produces MLR by a set formula – rounding up the average rate to the nearest ¼ p.c. and adding ½ p.c. In theory therefore MLR is merely a reflection of what is happening rather than affecting events. In practice the Bank of England has a couple of times intervened to push up the rate against the trend.

Taking it further back, the Treasury Bill rate is really produced by the supply and demand for money. That in turn is partly the result of international flows of cash, e.g. there may have been a large inflow of foreign money into London, or a panic about the state of sterling taking all the money out. So this goes further back to balance of payments which produces the expectations and confidence which bring money into Britain or encourage it to flow to healthier centres.

All of which gives an indication of the complex interrelated nature of the financial system, and how the policies of one country reverberate in another throughout its economy.

The MLR is published because that is the minimum the

Bank of England will charge to a borrower, such as a discount house, who therefore has more than a passing interest in how the rate moves. There is also the psychological effect of telling people just how the money market stands.

Monetarist

"History offers ample evidence that what determines the average level of prices and wages is the amount of money in the economy and not the greediness of business or workers." That is probably the most concise encapsulation of the monetarist view and comes from the arch priest of the cult, Professor Milton Friedman (in Capitalism and Freedom).

But if he is challenged, as still happens, he retreats enough to concede that "undoubtedly there can be and are influences running both ways", meaning that incomes can influence the quantity of money around as well as vice versa. But he and the monetarists maintain that the quantity of money is "an important independent influence" on economic fluctuations.

Opponents claim the relationships are not that causal and that governments must respond to demand for money, or substitutes will merely take its place. Lord Kaldor has shown that in Britain 74 p.c. of the deviation from long term money supply trends is caused by public sector deficits.

Money Supply

If you see frequent mentions of M1, M2, M3 on the City pages, it is not another example of motorway madness – these are just the different measures of how much money is floating round the economy. Professor Milton Friedman of Chicago calculated that inflation was a direct, though delayed, consequence of increasing money supply too quickly.

The problem then is to define what exactly is money – it is certainly more than just the cash in daily circulation. For instance, bank accounts contain money (though not in cash) and one person's balance is another overdraft and hence cash for some trader.

So M1 includes notes and coins in circulation plus the private sector sterling current accounts. M2 is hazy and not much used nowadays, and M3 is M1 plus other term deposits, which is mainly deposit accounts at banks, deposits at discount houses, and other accounts including public sector deposits.

As one would expect, normally M1 and M3 move in parallel, but recently there has been a divergence, some of which was explicable by the movements in interest rates, but some had experts frankly perplexed.

Monopoly

Two ways of making lots of money are to market a board game that stays popular for generations, and another is to control a market so completely that you can charge what you like. Both go under the name of Monopoly.

But the board game shows how words lose their meaning – it is about property development and not about monopoly at all. Strictly speaking a monopoly supplier is the one with no competitors, but British legislation has never taken the word literally and the Fair Trading Act 1973, Section 6 (i) reduced the official definition from a third to a quarter of the market.

This is probably more of an oligopoly with a small number of companies commanding most of the sales – such as detergent, sugar, newsprint, banking.

Often the power of a monopolist is diluted by the availability of alternatives. In any case in an age of international trade even if a company were the sole producer in one country, any attempt to exploit the situation would soon lead to foreign competition stepping in.

Worried people counter this reassurance by pointing to the swift growth of multinational companies which are coming to dominate some markets, and indeed some national economies. In fact though, multinationals are usually in fierce competition with each other – for instance General Motors and Ford are competing throughout the world, – and only IBM has anything like a world hold on a market.

And even IBM is experiencing an increasing amount of restriction. This is because it is still open to any country to limit the companies which operate within its boundaries and the multi-nationals have to be circumspect in the way they

MONOPOLY

resist for fear of incurring international odium. Not many companies would be prepared to take on such an overtly political role as did ITT in Chile, and considering the lambasting ITT has been getting over that even Harold Geneen might think twice in future.

In Britain most genuine monopolies are nationalized industries with legislation preventing competition, which is curious considering how fervently governments dislike private enterprise having a large share of any market.

Monopsony

Monopoly is a market in which there is only one supplier (e.g. railways, telephone service) but there are some markets in which there is only one buyer, and the economists have dubbed this monopsony. Predictably, such distortions of market economy are usually reserved for the unfettered strength of government and nationalized industry.

In theory international trade should reduce the government's buying power since its suppliers should be able to compete for foreign business, but the manufacturers are often so tied to the specifications set by the giant public sector purchases that when these are not accepable overseas (as the telephone exchange makers claim the Post Office eccentric buying policies are not), the power is well nigh absolute. It is further reinforced by the fact that these are usually sectors where all countries protect the home supplier.

Military equipment, including ships, is similarly afflicted, and some Labour governments have further aggravated the situation by preventing sales to countries with horrid governments.

Governments use their monopsony power to structure the supplying industry – airframes, aero engines, – and set not only product standards but often the profit rate as well.

National Economic Development Office

Selwyn Lloyd, Chancellor in 1961, decided that planning was a good idea. The government ought to talk to industrialists and trade union leaders to get an idea of where the country was going. The NED Council was born (NEDC, or Neddy) to bring senior ministers including the prime minister and the chancellor together with economists and union men and captains of industry.

For some time it was just a pleasant place to chat. But in 1964 the Labour government got enthusiastic about planning and used Neddy as the medium for producing a National Plan. Very soon the Neddy economists experienced in these things were snatched away to George Brown's Department of Economic Affairs, after which NEDO tried to edge out of the whole adventure.

The ignominious failure of the National Plan's 4 p.c. growth target (because the planners had forgotten about balance of payments constraints) brought all attempts at planning into disrepute.

With its original raison d'etre brought into disrepute, the NEDO put its main effort behind the Little Neddies. These were committees formed to look after a range of industries, and like the big Neddy consist of senior managers, trade union leaders, an independent chairman and are serviced by the NED Office. These committees try to improve the standard of their industries by educating them. They publish a vast range of booklets on everything from manpower wastage to the economic prospects several years ahead.

National Institute for Economic and Social Research

Peering into the future has become big business in the past few years but still the NIESR quarterly projections of the trends in the UK economy are accorded more respect than most. The body was set up in 1938 as a non-profit making research centre and has had close contact with the Treasury in its compilation and manipulation of a computer-based model of the British economy.

Although the approaches tend to be similar, the results the

two produce are different. Most people think the institute is consistently too optimistic but they have been carefully combing their figures for regular – and hence correctable – error.

Nobody is ever quite right but then there are several reasons why this might be impossible. As has often been pointed out, the statistics these forecasters use are already several months out of date when they get them – and that includes the Treasury itself – so it has been likened to driving a car while gazing through the rear window.

Another problem is that by the predicted time the government's policies have changed the circumstances so the actual forecasts can not be gauged to be true or false – uttering them changed the situation.

In view of the fact that economies seem inherently unpredictable, it is surprising that the NIESR or the Treasury, or the forecasts produced by the papers, get even as near the truth as they do.

Non-Voting

Some public companies issue two sets of ordinary shares – often designated. A and B – and voting rights are sometimes restricted to only one of the sets, usually the smaller set. The idea is to maintain control of the company in the hands of a small group of people, often the men who owned the company before it went public.

It is not done often and the Stock Exchange does not take kindly to the disenfranchisement of shareholders and presumably one would only buy to get a share in a very good investment, where one had considerable confidence in the continuing efficiency and good faith of the management.

Oligopoly

Genuine monopolies are rare – it is far more usual for a small number of companies to control a market. Yet people talk about monopolists who are not, and the Monopolies and Mergers Commission can examine any company with more than 25 p.c. of the market. These situations are often referred to as near-monopolies or almost monopolies. The term for a few outfits cornering a market is oligopoly.

Examples of this are clearing banks where National Westminster, Barclays, Lloyds, and Midland have practically the whole branch banking system sewn up between them; detergents where Procter and Gamble, and Unilever are dominant; petrol, with Shell, BP, Exxon (or Esso) and Gulf commanding the market, though there are still half a dozen with minor shares; and cigarettes with Imperial Gallaher, and Rothman.

Options

The option as a means of minimizing losses at times of price fluctuations was known as far back as the 16th century. The practice can be used both as a form of protection for securities you hold and as a gamble on shares you might want to buy.

If you own some equities and there is a likelihood that through a cash shortage in the near future you may want to sell them, you may want to be reasonably sure that the price will not have tumbled disastrously in the interim. So you arrange a put option which in effect is a contact which gives you the right to sell the shares within the next three months at a stated price (the striking price) which is usually the price of the shares on the day you arrange the deal.

You naturally have to pay for the service but that can be considered insurance money. If the price does drop and you do have to sell it will have been worth it, if not you have only lost the option money.

Conversely if you are pretty sure a company's share price will rise substantially you can buy a call option and so within the next three months at a time of steep increase you can still buy at the price prevailing on the day of your contract and then sell at a handsome profit. Once again, if you are wrong, the loss is still limited to the option money. It used to be considered a comparatively cheap way of sticking your neck out and dealing in the things you do not own but in recent years the cost has risen substantially. There is also the double option.

Ordinary Shares

These are often known as equities. Another way of looking at ordinary shares is to say that the owner of the company (shareholder) is protected in that his maximum loss is the value of his shares and is not liable to the full extent of the company's indebtedness. Hence the name of limited company. There are preferred ordinary shares (see Preference) and deferred ordinaries which come near the bottom in the order of priorities for payment, after preferred.

Organization for Economic Co-operation and Development

The rich nations' research and chat club which was set up in December 1960 as a wider based successor to the Organization for European Economic Co-operation. The convention itself was intended to 'promote policies designed to achieve the highest sustainable economic growth and employment and a rising standard of living in member countries, while maintaining financial stability, and thus contribute to the development of the world economy; to contribute to sound economic expansion in member as well as non-member countries in the process of economic development; to contribute to the expansion of world trade on a multilateral, non-discriminatory basis in accordance with international obligations.'

High aims. In fact it spends a lot of time examining and co-ordinating statistics provided by members, and publishing studies prognosticating about the economies of the member countries. In the past some of these have issued some dire and well-merited warnings about the direction the UK economy was taking.

OECD also publishes booklets on a wide range of other esoteric topics from educational policies to the infrastructure for regional development, fisheries and tourism.

The members are Australia, Austria, Belgium, Britain, Canada, Denmark, Finland, France, West Germany, Greece, Iceland, Ireland, Italy, Japan, Luxembourg, Netherlands, New Zealand, Norway, Portugal, Spain, Sweden, Switzerland, Turkey and the United States.

Paper Gold

It just shows how far we are from ridding ourselves from the tyranny of gold and from the emotional reaction that it still remains the only criterion of value, that when new forms of wealth are discovered they are still related to the yellow metal.

At various times first coal and then oil have been called black gold, and when special drawing rights (qv) were invented they were immediately dubbed paper gold.

Parities

Just another term for rates of exchange (i.e. the value of one currency in terms of another). These are fixed by the simple process of supply and demand which in turn is affected by the confidence in a country's economic situation.

If its inflation is faster than anybody else's or if the prices of its goods are uncompetitive then either it has to introduce some drastic measures at home or devalue (or float) which will provide a new parity. Deviation of 2¼ p.c. either side of a fixed parity is permissible by international agreement.

P/E Ratio

There are several different measures of whether a company's shares are a bargain or not and a commonly used one is the ratio of price to earnings.

In essence this tells you two things: how highly regarded is the company by other investors, and at the current rates how many years' profit you have had to pay for in purchasing the shares. So if the shares sell for 40p and the net earnings per share are 4p then the price/earnings is 10.

An advantage of this is that it is used in both Britain and the United States so you can directly compare investments on this basis.

Petrodollars

The surplus cash oil exporters have sloshing around in their coffers has been dubbed petrodollars. Basically this is the money the countries have received for their oil but have not spent on imports – because there just is not that much they can import or perhaps because there just are not enough of them.

The amount varied with price and the volume of oil sold but certainly topped $50,000 million. And fortunately for Britain with its tragic balance of payments, about a third was placed in the U.K. Another 20 p.c. went to the US, another third to other countries, and the rest to international agencies. And in 1974 'oil-exporting countries financed the largest part of the UK current account deficit by adding £2,200 million to their sterling holdings.'

Of course, since the oil exporters (not just Arabs but also Nigerians, Venezuelans and Indonesians) also put their money into Japan, there are petroyens, and in Switzerland there are petrofrancs, and so on. But as the oil tends to be invoiced and quoted in dollars, petrodollars it is.

Since most of the money is on short call it has not helped industry much, which does not need a lot of cash during a time of recession anyway. The recession incidentally is partly caused by that amount of cash being taken out of world trade.

Phillips Curve

Professor A. W. Phillips looked back at wages and employment figures for the years between 1861 and 1957 and came to the conclusion that workers got larger pay rises when unemployment was small than when it was large.

In other words when workers became scarce companies were prepared to bid higher to get some. Conversely as unemployment rose the wage rises became smaller until there was a theoretical level when pay increases would stop – any more unemployment beyond that point would mean wages actually falling.

The line which shows this on a graph is called the Phillips curve.

From this it follows that if excessive wage demands at times of high employment are causing inflation, and the government cannot get the unions to reduce claims, the way to stem the inflationary spiral is to increase unemployment. This course was repeatedly advocated by numerous economists, including Professor Frank Paish, for years.

But since 1969 unemployment has come and gone without any noticeable softening of union attitudes, partly perhaps because wage demands are more a fuction of the strength of the unions than of the demand for labour. So Sir Kenneth Berrill, chief economic adviser to the Treasury, concluded that the rate of pay inflation is insensitive to the level of unemployment 'over quite a wide band'; and the National Institute for Economic and Social Research concurred (March 1975), 'there is no way of knowing the scale of unemployment required to produce any given change in the inflation rate'. But in the United States the point at which wage inflation becomes zero has been estimated to be between 5 p.c. and 10 p.c. unemployment, and the UK has not moved far into that bracket.

Placing

There are five ways of issuing shares. In a private placing all the shares available from a company are issued to one or a group of financial institutions such as pension funds, insurance companies and investments trusts.

In this case the company need not be quoted. They tell the jobber they are prepared to buy and he allots them the shares. As soon as the Stock Exchange Council has given permission to deal they get the equities and dealings can start.

This can also happen as part of a Stock Exchange introduction (one of the other methods of issuing shares) when a company comes to the market for the first time. In that case part or all the shares offered can be taken up by the institutions or even by the issuing house itself.

The other methods of issuing shares are a public issue complete with prospectus and underwriters, and a rights issue giving existing shareholders in a quoted company the opportunity to buy more – as the terms are usually favourable the quotas are usually taken up if only to resell soon after.

Preference Shares

These are fixed interest shares whose holders rank immediately after debentures (if issued) for their dividends and so come before the holders of ordinary shares. If the cash is not enough to pay dividends it can be carried forward for almost any number of years on cumulative shares.

The holders also get similar priority for repayment if the company is wound up, but usually preference shareholders have no vote at company meetings.

Quotas

In the context of macroeconomics or international trade the word is usually used to refer to a way of restricting imports. It imposes a ceiling on the amount shipped in, to protect either the home industry or the currency. In the goods subject to the limitation each seller country may have a set amount it can sell in a year, and if it reaches this after a week it will just have to do without any trade for the other 51 weeks.

The system is understandably disliked by the seller countries which usually negotiate for the removal of quotas. And GATT does not like them and is against their being imposed.

Quotation

Permission to buy and sell a company's shares is granted by the Stock Exchange Council only after the company has met strict requirements. The rules for admission to quotation are lengthy and rigorous as the Council and the City Panel are careful to police their own parish to pre-empt outside interference.

Americans often refer to it as listing.

Recession

In the world of economics you first get a plateau, then a decline, then a recession, then a depression, and finally a slump. So a recession is nasty without being really horrid. The arguments usually centre on, at least between politicians, when one expression shades into another. It does not really matter.

Another difference between a recession and a slump is that a slump is a catastrophic collapse from which no salvation seems visible, while a recession can be seen to be a temporary set-back and one which need not necessarily stop the longer term investments.

Reflation

This is a way of trying to perk up a sluggish economy by injecting a bit of consumer demand. It can be done by monetary means like encouraging the banks to borrow and lend more money, and removing restrictions which often prevent them going as far along with this sort of policy as they would like.

Or the Chancellor can use fiscal measures like cutting taxes (such as readucing the rate of VAT, or lowering income tax) or abolishing hire purchase deposits. Another way of stimulating demand of some sort is by just getting more money circulating in the economy – increasing old age pensions usually does this as most pensioners are so hard pressed that they usually spend any increase straight away.

With more money around and more people buying, production increases and if the manufacturers see any prospect that the upturn will continue they will increase their investment in capital equipment and increase production. All this of course generates yet more employment and so more money and so further reflation.

What has often happened in the past is that reflation has increased demand which could not be met by home manufacturers and so two things happened – prices and imports rose. The resultant inflation and adverse balance of payments caused the Chancellor to damp down demand (disinflation and deflation) and so we had the stop-go cycle.

Relative Price Effect

This confusing term has been cropping up with increasing frequency into the arguments about public expenditure. It is in fact the difference between inflation in the public sector and that in the country as a whole. The public part is measured by using five basic price indices relevant to that area, and then relating them to the general rate of inflation, which for some obscure reason is not measured by the retail price index. Instead they use the gross domestic product factor cost price index, known to its friends as the gdp deflator.

There is actually a permanent RPE increase quite apart from the distorting effects of inflation. The public sector increase is about 0.6 p.c. a year, or some 2.5 p.c. over the five year span of a rolling-forward public spending plan. This is due to the rise in real personal incomes – earnings since the war have as a general rule risen faster than prices and since the public sector with its army of civil servants (and its army) has a higher than average labour content, its costs rise faster than those for industry.

This is one of the reasons public expenditure calculations are so vulnerable to wage increases. But there are other factors affecting RPE as well. In the 1971–1975 period some £1,700m more was spent than was forecast as a result of public sector costs rising very much faster than inflation and faster than anticipated. The vast majority of this was due to land and construction costs.

Reserves

Otherwise known as official reserves or even more grandiloquently as gold and convertible currency reserves. This is the cache of 'cash' in the Bank of England vaults which fluctuates but is composed of gold bars, special drawing rights, credits at the International Monetary Fund, and convertible currency mostly in United States dollars with gold and dollars being the major items.

These reserves are a sort of national equivalent to a current bank account for foreign trade. The total gives some clue to the nation's economic health, especially since it accrues not only from trade but from the deposits in the UK by foreign lenders and hence indicates their confidence in the country. But like all current accounts it is by no means the whole picture.

Just as a person may have deposit accounts and own property, so Britain has a range of assets including holdings at other countries' central banks and overseas property.

But where does the money come from? Well, let us say an Arab prince decides he likes the interest rates in London and wants to put around a few hundred million dollars into a London bank. Banks are allowed to hold a certain amount of foreign currency for day to day transactions but beyond a certain limit, the foreign money goes into the Bank of England which puts the dollars into its exchange equalisation account from which it pays the bank the dollars' equivalent in sterling.

Another source is the overseas borrowing by the government and public enterprises. Another activity affecting the level of reserves is the Bank of England's moves to stabilize sterling's exchange rate. If there is brisk demand for trading in sterling because several international business transactions must be settled, the Bank sells; if sterling is weak, the Bank buys for other currencies.

And of course if foreigners invest in British assets (e.g. Treasury Bills, or the Kuwait Investment Office's purchase of St Martins Property) they use foreign currency and that too ends up in the Bank's capacious vaults (if only metaphorically). The state of the balance of trade will also obviously affect it since UK goods are paid for in foreign money while the British must pay for imports in dollars, francs, yen, Deutschemarks and so on.

Reverse Yield Gap

It was generally assumed that equities should yield more than government securities since the risk is greater, but in recent years this reasonable assumption has been overturned and gilt edged have been producing higher returns. The difference of the two is the yield gap, and since the trend seems upside down, when the gilts yield more it is called a reverse yield gap. The gap is actually between the average yield on the FT 30 share index, and 2½ p.c. Consols.

One of the reasons the gap reversed was that inflation started accelerating interest rates and that caused the price of fixed interest securities to fall. People expected the trend to continue and so discounted the possibility of capital losses. Coupled with this was the expectation that dividends from companies would roughly keep pace with inflation.

The result was that people bought equities even though the yield was lower, and this was part of the general assumption that investment in shares provided a medium term hedge against inflation.

Rights Issue

This is a distribution of shares in a fixed proportion to existing shareholders in a company according to the size of their original holding. The issue is made at a given price, usually below that prevailing in the market and is a convenient way for a company to raise additional cash or reduce its short term borrowings. Should the shareholder not want to take up the rights he may, of course, dispose of them through normal stock exchange channels.

Scrip Issue

Companies sometimes issue extra shares to existing holders for no extra cash. This may seem generous but is in fact little more than window dressing or a book-keeping exercise. One reason is that as a company ploughs back some of its profits and increases its reserves, it gets a steadily increasing income and so the dividend as a percentage begins to look embarrassingly high.

If companies were seen to be paying 60 p.c. dividends there might well be mutterings about greedy capitalists, despite the fact that the share price would be steadily raised to ensure that the yield on an investor's money would not be out of line.

This is a smokescreen. For the company it just capitalises reserves, and so just transfers the money from one line to another in accounts. Reasonably enough the share price is immediately adjusted since the mere issuing of paper makes no difference to the financial position of the company. So on a one for one issue (each holder gets the same number of shares he holds, to end up with double the number he originally held) the price is halved. But this too helps the company since too high a share price may keep it out of the hands of the average investor.

Seasonal Adjustments

There are lies, damned lies, statistics, and seasonally adjusted figures. Government statistics are usually issued in two forms – the straight figures, and then the figures adjusted by the so called smoothing factor which purports to remove the regularly recurring seasonal variations and so show whether the change is a true one or merely a reflection of the normal movement at the time of year. Sometimes of course they only provide seasonally adjusted index numbers, and then heaven knows what the figures mean.

In fact the adjustments tend to add almost as much confusion as they remove. Take housing. Normally building activity declines in the winter during the worst ice, snow and cold, and then recovers sharply as spring begins to thaw things out. But what about a very warm winter when it is pleasanter than some of the June days we have had? And what about the rebound effect that is supposed to result from the slow period – will it happen?

Given the fact that every year seems to introduce its own crop of strikes or other disruptions, how comparable is one with another? Still the Central Statistical Office beavers away in a desperate attempt to make the welter of figures mean something, so it seems almost churlish to complain that one is being confused.

Secured

This is the safer sort of investment because a specific piece of property is charged against the loan so the lender – investor – in fact holds the mortgage for some of the company property. Conversely, unsecured notes or loan stock are acknowledgments of debts and promissory notes with any specific assets being charged against the money. So the investor merely has a general claim against the assets of a company.

When an outfit goes bust people who hold unsecured notes are obviously further down the line to be repaid, and as the company will presumably already be deeply in debt by the time it goes under, there is only a small chance of getting repaid, while the secured creditors are more certain of their cash.

Slump

A disastrous and long term economic downturn which is recognized by high unemployment, low profits, falling production and low consumption. In the true sense of the word there has not been one since the end of the 1920s, partly as a result of the analysis and advice of Lord Keynes.

Following the wielding of the Arab oil power there was the fear that the consequent major deficit by most of the industrialized countries might provoke them into restrictive actions to improve their balance of payments. This could have led to a steadily aggravated decrease in world trade which might well lead to a slump.

But the lesson had been well learned and most countries

acted with a restrained responsibility that was refreshing.

Slumpflation

As the country's finance continues to do unprecedented things (going through contortions economists have long deemed impossible) these learned men must coin neologisms to encompass the new phenomena. So we have slumpflation, stagflation and so on.

It was always considered axiomatic that industrial booms resulted in high rates of inflation and slumps led to disinflation. But despite this self-evident truth being taught in universities for a century the economy has managed to produce a stagnant industrial output simultaneously with high rates of inflation.

This becomes less surprising when you realize that inflation can have many causes and the government can take many steps to control it.

Slumpflation in this context is defined as a depressed national economy with falling production and investment, coupled with a high rate of inflation.

Smithsonian Agreement

In December, 1971, there was a strenuous effort to bring order into the world currency situation and organize a wholesale realignment of the rates of exchange to tidy up the piecemeal devaluations and fixed the rates themselves, taking into account differential rates of exchange and heaven knows what.

It was a laudable and hard working attempt and within a year or so was completely vitiated. First to spoil the pretty picture was Britain by floating its currency in June, 1972, and since then several other countries have followed suit.

Countries have become disinclined to exert the painful discipline which the maintenance of a fixed exchange rate entailed. They may have avoided the rising rates of unemployment and the unpleasant stop-go cycles such strictness needed, but are probably getting the compensating disadvantage now of world wide high inflation. Even freedom has a price.

Snake in the Tunnel

The Smithsonian agreement widened the limits of permissible fluctuations of one currency against another. In the case of a fixed parity of, let us say, 200 cowrie shells to the dollar as the rate of exchange, it could move 2¼ p.c. either side – from 204½ to 195½ cowrie shells to the dollar. This was the tunnel. It was 4½ p.c. wide from top to bottom with the dollar as a line down the centre.

The European countries decided as a first step towards economic integration to bring their own currencies into greater harmony by saying that in addition to this, their own currencies could not move more than 1⅛ p.c. either side of parity relative to each other. This was the snake. It was 2¼ p.c. wide and it wriggled down the tunnel. If the top of the snake (the strongest European currency inside it) touched the top of the tunnel then the belly (the weakest currency) would be along the par line with the dollar.

To maintain this tight discipline the member governments had to intervene to help currencies which threatened to break out of the snake. So if a currency was about to burst the belly, the other countries, would support by buying. In return the supported country had to buy its currency back at a later date with its reserves of gold and hard currency.

But countries jibbed at this, especially when the cost began to get high enough seriously to deplete their gold reserves, and Britain, France, Ireland, Italy and Austria all dropped out of the snake. The snake survived but only just. Yet when it was first proposed it was hoped gradually to slim the snake as the 1980 target for integration approached.

Social Wage

One of Mr Denis Healey's more questionable inventions was the social wage – the splendid services we all derive from the benevolence of the state and which he urges us to count in our calculations of what we receive.

It comes in the form of social security, education, food subsidies, libraries, health services, transport subsidies, housing, etc., and totals £1,000 a working head, according to Mr

Joel Barnett, chief secretary to the Treasury (*Hansard*, April 22, 1975).

The Minister may well be right to remind us we are getting these services, but they are certainly not free, for this is what we pay taxes for.

If you add up income taxes (including corporation tax), National Insurance and National Health contributions, redundancy fund payments and taxes on expenditure (tobacco, cars, alcohol, VAT, etc.), in 1975 it came to £33,229 million. Divide that by the working population of around 25 million and each one on average pays some £1,329 for the £1,000 of social wage.

Thank you, Mr Healey.

Special Drawing Rights

A new type of international money was dreamed up in 1969 to try to lubricate trade without having to rely on a constant large outflow of American dollars. It was also the latest attempt to get away from the anachronistic reliance by sophisticated bankers off such antiquated means of exhange as lumps of yellow metal.

The move got impetus from a realization that the rate of increase in international trade would always have to be paralleled by a similar growth in gold mining. Neither the ability nor the continuous willingness of the two major gold producers – South Africa and Russia – could be relied on for ever. Nevertheless the mystique remained and the value of SDR was fixed in terms of gold at the nice round figure of 0.888671 grams. Subsequently however it was defined in terms of other currencies.

SDRs are essentially lines of credit opened for countries by the International Monetary Fund (qv) to help them settle overseas debts. The purpose was that temporary embarrassments from payments deficits might be bridged over, though the IMF was always insistent that SDRs are no alternative to getting the balance of payments right.

The special part of the name is to differentiate the scheme from ordinary IMF drawing rights available to all members.

Spot Rate

This is the rate of exchange for a currency (or the price of a commodity) for purchasing and paying on the spot. As opposed to forward buying, which is paying today's price for delivery of a currency or a commodity at some specified time in the future, say three months hence. But the forward rate will obviously be different from the spot rate and will depend on how the traders see the prices moving during the period in question. And also on the prevailing interest rates.

Through an astute use of the forward or futures market, businessmen can provide a protection against exchange rates moving against them during the period of a contract.

Spread

The buying and selling prices of shares and unit trust units differ – occasionally by subtantial amounts. For shares the difference covers the costs (and risks) of the jobber, but for unit trusts the difference – or spread – is even wider. The reason is that offer price (at which trust managers sell to the public) includes the initial management charge while the bid price (at which managers repurchase units) is calculated by dividing the value of the fund by the number of units, minus the cost of selling the shares. So unit price spread is often up to 5 p.c., and occasionally slightly more.

Stag

Capel Court by the Stock Exchange was called Stag Alley during the last century. That was the time of the railway mania, and down there prospered a special breed of Alley Men who were sharp enough to get the allotment letters of the new shares of railway companies first, and then hurried nimbly along the street to cash in on their good fortune.

Similarly nowadays a stag is a man who subscribes for new issues only to make a quick profit as soon as dealings begin and prices rise above the issue.

As popular issues are usually over-subscribed and a ballot decides who will succeed, experienced stags contrive to send in more than one application form, though there have been attempts to stop this practice.

Stocks and Shares

The investor is in effect lending his money to companies and governments in return for an IOU (a certificate) and a rate of interest. (This is not a legal, just a convenient, definition.) But there is a wide range of conditions attached to the loan, and a correspondingly large number of names for the IOUs and transactions.

Although in conversation (and sometimes in newspapers) the two words are used interchangeably, there is a difference between stocks and shares. Stocks are usually quoted per £100 nominal value, though fractions of this are also dealt in. Some examples are government stocks, corporation stocks, debentures and so on.

In addition to this market a limited company issues a set number of certificates with a nominal or par value, say 5p or 10p, or 50p or £1. These are called shares. Unlike stocks these are not divisible – you can buy around £100 worth (depending on how near the prevailing price approximates) or you can buy a set number like 500 shares.

Supporting a Currency

In the days of fixed currency parities inevitably one of them would from time to time weaken as its country's economy began to look dubious to the rest of the world. If the country in question felt the problems were temporary or for some reason disliked the idea of devaluation it could try and jack up the value of its money. The long term way was by removing the problems which had caused the weakness in the first place, but in the short term something had to be done to prevent the currency being unacceptable at the official rate of exchange.

So the country supported it. The usual way of doing this was for the central bank (in Britain the Bank of England) to buy its own currency. So the Bank would spend the gold and dollar reserves buying sterling and since these things respond to supply and demand, the value of sterling would rise. This becomes especially true of major international currencies since people have to have them for some overseas transactions.

SUPPORTING A CURRENCY

This sort of thing could be fine as a short term measure if it worked. But if there was little sign of the underlying faults being cured the hard earned gold and dollars would just drain away leaving the currency as pallid as ever. If that happened countries imposed drastic deflation or devalued. The practice lingers as central banks, e.g. the Bank of England, try to prevent floating currencies weakening too fast or at inopportune moments.
(See also devaluation, floating currency)

Swap Arrangements
The reserves of a country consist of gold and other countries' currency so by swapping currencies two countries increase their reserves and so in theory strengthen the backing for their own currencies. Sounds almost too easy doesn't it?

The process was invented in fact to prevent speculators from knocking over a currency which did not really deserve to go down but which was temporarily going through a too weak a position to withstand a concerted attack by wealthy speculators. In other words it did not have adequate reserves to support the home currency.

In that case the central banks of other countries with which it has these arrangements transfer enough money to allow purchase of its currency lavishly enough to exhaust the speculators' resources. When they have spent all their money selling the currency short and eventually find they need the money for ordinary transactions, they have to buy it back at higher prices and the tide, or rather the ebb, has been stemmed. The central bank can even make a profit on the deal.

Britain has arrangements with 12 major industrialized countries who will come to her aid when her own resources run dry.

Terms of Trade

This is an indicator of how hard we have to work for our foreign exchange. The comparison of imports and exports by price is the terms of trade. So if the general price of imports rises faster than the price of exports, the terms of trade are becoming less favourable – that is we are having to work harder and make more goods to be able to buy the same amount of foreign produce.

Understandably enough, the other phrase for this is that terms of trade are moving against us. And of course vice versa.

In Britain the indicator is calculated by dividing the index of export prices by the index of import prices and multiplying by 100. So a fall in the final index indicates an adverse movement.

Tips and Taps

The Stock Exchange has certain similarities with horse racing. You put your money on past form bearing in mind what the course (state of the economy) may be like, and paying particular attention to trainer and jockey (chairman and managing director). And as on the courses there are tipsters though in the City they *should* be rather more sophisticated and better informed.

But it is always worth asking why somebody should let you in on a deal which will shorten the odds (or push up the share price) and with equal validity one can ask: 'If you're so smart why aren't you rich?'

A tap is a situation where someone has a large holding he wants to get rid of but is waiting for the right price. Hence the cynical comment: 'where there is a tip there is a tap'. In other words City men are seldom altruists.

Trades Union Congress

The central organization for the majority of trade unions. About 140 unions are members, covering about 10,000,000 of the 25,000,000 total working population of Britain. For those with less pronounced political sympathies a rival organization called Confederation of Independent Staff Organizations has been set up.

Treasury Bill

Not a man called William who runs the economy. This is the way the government raises the short term cash needed to carry on the running of the country. Each week about £100 million worth of Treasury Bills are offered for sale by tender. The Treasury promises to repay each Bill at the par of £100 in three months' time so the discount houses and banks who put in their bids, pitch their offer price to cover the expected rate of effective interest in the money market.

That is if the tender is at £98 the rate of interest is 8 p.c. a year (£2 equals 2 p.c. for the quarter year making 8 p.c. per annum). Everybody tenders separately and the Bank of England runs its finger down the list of tenders until it reaches the lowest acceptable bid, or runs out of bills. So one can see that the interest on Treasury Bills both reflects and influences the prevailing rate of interest in the money market.

Underwriting

The underwriter of a stock or share issue is the man who guarantees that the company (or local authority) gets the funds it needs whether the public wants to buy the shares or not. If, say, the certificates are printed, the prospectus prepared, the issue advertisements placed, and 24 hours before the start of applications gilt edged prices fall, a local authority stock could suddenly look distinctly unattractive. And all sorts of things can intervene to ruin the chances of an equity issue.

When that sort of disaster happens, the merchant banks and the like who are the normal underwriters and who in the past have been making a tidy fortune from rock-solid underwriting, suddenly start earning their keep. They are left with the shares that nobody wants, and since on news of the failure the price will sag, they can either hang in the hope of better times to come and thus immobilize their cash, or sell at a loss.

This may partly be the reason issues are usually set at attractive prices.

There are of course also Lloyds underwriters who take a share of insurance risks. That is a different institution and arrangement.

Unemployment

There are an awful lot of ifs and buts about the unemployment figures, especially if you start trying to make international comparisons. The farther you look into the statistics the more difficult it becomes to make dogmatic statements about them.

For instance it looks as if the hard core of idle unemployables is a lot softer than people thought. The Department of Employment asked its offices to classify the register into categories ranging from qualified and eager to work, down to disinclined to work and with poor prospects. Six months later two thirds of the top category had found jobs, but a third of the people in the bottom category had also done so. So even the gloomy forebodings of the Department staff were wrong.

And just who is counted? Well, at Easter some 90,000 higher education students signed on in the hope of getting supplementary benefits (not having paid stamps they are not eligible for the dole). But women are generally not in the lists. A 1971 household survey found 230,000 women looking for work but not on the register, and the following year's census counted 150,000 of them.

This may be one reason why American figures are higher than the UK. The count is taken on sample surveys (which therefore hide regional variations) and this will include women who are looking for jobs, no matter how desultory and intermittent the search is.

The British figures also omit a large number of men looking for work but not signing on for dole. In 1972 there were 70,000 of them. On the other hand the figures do include 50,000 early retirements signing on to avoid paying NHS stamps and so on, though with little prospect of finding work.

Also included are about 50,000 disabled who also would find it hard to get jobs. And the total also includes all those signing on for the benefits even though they may have only a week or a fortnight between jobs. There may be as many as 300,000 of these. But even all these figures are suspect since most of them are estimates.

Given that there is so much estimating and guessing it is dangerous to attach too much significance to small movements – they maybe within the margin of error – and even more hazardous to compare international rates of unemployment.

Unit of Account

The Common Market does so many international money calculations that it has invented a non-existent new money called the unit of account as a sort of EEC supranational currency. There are 16 areas in which the UA is used and most of the definitions are different. For the Commission budget, the unit is defined in terms of all EEC currencies at their Smithsonian (qv) rates of exchange, unweighted by the country's importance or trade.

Another definition fixed the value with a charming simplicity at 0.88867088 grams of fine gold. A nice round figure which should make everything so much easier. In fact it is not quite as silly as at first it sounds since that was the value of the US dollar when it was pegged to gold in the Bretton Woods system (qv). The dollar is not what it was but the EEC is obviously still afflicted with nostalgia.

The common agricultural policy, on the other hand, uses UAs which are a mixture of Smithsonian parities, the rates of exchange of currencies in the snake (qv), and the floating rates for other currencies (though not the true floating rate but the relation to the 'snake' currencies which is decided after inter-governmental negotiation). It is the rate of exchange between this UA and sterling which is the Green Pound (qv).

The European Coal and Steel Community uses a UA based on 6 month average value on a weighted scale, the development fund uses another UA and the statistical office yet another. Then there is the so called 'basket of currencies' rate related to the weighted member currencies: Deutschemarks 27.3 p.c., sterling 17.5 p.c., French franc 19.5 p.c. and the Lira 14 p.c., and so on.

The Commission seems unperturbed by this bewildering range of definitions and produces a sort of teleological argument that the use to which the UA is put should be allowed to determine the definition – some need to be more flexible or up to date than others In that case perhaps we should use the words with lower case initial letters and so refer back to the economists' four functional definitions of money: medium of exchange, store of value, basis of credit, and unit of accunt (i.e. measure of value).

Unit Trust

A unit trust is an excellent way for the small saver to spread his investments and so prevent being stuck with the shares of an unsuccessful company. As with investment trusts there is the added advantage of having full time professionals look after the investing.

The difference however is that unit trusts are not quoted

UNIT TRUST

companies and the market in them exists because the trust managers buy and sell them. The price of a unit (allowing for the usual spread or difference between buying and selling price) is linked to the value of the shares held by the trust.

If the stock market as a whole goes up generally the price of the units can be expected to move in sympathy, though if the managers are competent the price of the units should drop less in a bear market than the FT Index. In a bull market they should out-pace the Index.

Usury

For all those who have been saying rude words like this to building societies, bank managers and hire purchase companies, here is the true definition – and possibly proof that you were right.

After the ninetheenth-century usury laws were repealed in 1854 to provide greater flow of capital to industry, a new Moneylenders Act was brought in to regulate the rate of interest which could be charged. It said that anything over 48 p.c. a year was unreasonable and if anybody lent money at, say, 50 p.c., the burden of proof was on him to show that the circumstances made it reasonable.

This has not, of course, prevented exorbitant interest being charged, and with the current accelerating rates it is possible that a number of people actually have fallen into the hands of the usurers. Thank heavens the Fleet Prison for debtors is no more.

Value at Par

This is the face value of a particular share – say 10p, 20p, 50p or £1. It bears little relation to anything, since it is probably not related to the asset value and seldom much to do with the share price prevailing.

In the case of government stocks though, nominal or par value is the amount at which they will be redeemed, so there the amount is significant. There are also no-par-value shares in the United States – the equities have been given no face value and the price is determined purely by the stock exchange.

Voluntary Restraint

This is usually similar to the army way of getting volunteers, I want three volunteers, you, you and you. So voluntary restraint means people quite voluntarily hold back pay demands, price increases, profit margins, etc., and if they did not the government would batter them over the head.

Actually, to be fair this depends on what is being restrained. Voluntary restraint of wage demands can mean asking for 45 p.c. wage rise instead of 50 p.c.

The drug companies exercise voluntary restraint in the prices they charge the National Health Service for their medicines, but when Hoffman La Roche considered the level it was being asked to restrain itself to was too low for comfort and refused, the Department of Health got a parliamentary order to hit them with.

Wall Street

This is one of those semi-mythical places like Whitehall, Harley Street, Carnaby Street ... a convenient label for a jumble of ideas. Generally it means the New York Stock Exchange which is on the corner of Wall Street and Broad Street. Another name for this exchange is the Big Board, and although there are many other stock exchanges in America it accounts for the vast majority of trading – perhaps 85 p.c.

In New York there is also the American Stock Exchange. In addition there is over the counter trading in non-quoted companies, which means that security dealers buy and sell the shares over the telephone.

World Bank

Its proper name is the International Bank for Reconstruction and Development and it is one of the two survivors of the 1944 Bretton Woods agreement (qv) (the other is the International Monetary Fund). The Fund is actually a bank, and the World Bank is actually a fund.

The idea was that the World Bank would provide capital to help companies reconstruct their economies after the ravages of the war. Beyond that the bank is there to help member countries in their development through lending to government agencies (or even private enterprises if no other sources of cash is available) or by guaranteeing private loans.

Loans are usually for 15 to 20 years and the bank has become one of the major routes of multi-lateral aid, with the capital coming from the developed world. The sort of project which would interest the Bank would be agriculture, hydro-electric schemes, agricultural modernization, port improvements, etc.

XD, XC, XR

Shortly after the announcement by a company of its dividend the shares are quoted ex-dividend. This means that the old holder is still on the company's shareholder register and any buyer would not be getting the dividend. The usual abbreviation is xd.

Similarly if a company makes a scrip issue the prices are normally quoted ex-capitalization (abbreviated xc) on the day after the allotment letters are posted to existing holders.

Sometimes a company also offers existing shareholders the right to buy more shares and once again the shares are sold without this right after the offer has been posted off (abbreviation for this is xr).

Yen

What would financial alphabets do without the yen? It is the unit of Japanese money which not so long ago was thought the safest, soundest and all-conquering. Now that even Japan has suffered very rapid inflation, massive wage demands and even devaluation, everybody breathes a sigh of relief.

It is probably premature. Though by all accounts the Japanese are choking themselves almost to death with the effluents from their humming industry, and though they have been badly hit by the oil problems and wage increases, their rate of growth may still be double that of Britain in a good year.

Yield

One way of assessing a share is by its yield. The gross yield is a percentage return you would get on your money if you bought at the price calculated. If Shell yields 4.3 p.c. then every £100 invested in the company would bring in £4.30 before tax.

This is obviously important for investors interested in income but of less concern to those who are buying for capital appreciation, and in fact a general feeling that the company is going to do exceedingly well (and so shoot its share price up) will usually be discounted and therefore produce a fairly low yield.

The conclusion is therefore that the Stock Exchange expects great things of companies with a low yield but the high yielders leave people more dubious.

To work it out for yourself multiply the annual percentage dividend by the nominal value of the share and then divide is by the current price. This is called the gross or current yield. The earnings yield is the same thing except that it takes earnings rather than dividends.

Z-Account

This is a privileged account held at the Bank of England by certain financial institutions such as gilt-edged jobbers, discount houses and insurance companies. It enables them to certify and register gilt-edged stock transfers over the counter thereby speeding up the whole process, which in the case of a private individual dealing in gilt-edged securities takes three or four days. It is a privilege not enjoyed by many.

Zollverein

The earliest harbinger of a common market – the German word for customs union. The first one was established as far back as 1833 between Prussia and the then independent German states. They agreed to abolish all tariffs between each other and erect a common external tariff wall instead.

It was a similar theory that over a century later created the Common Market and the European Free Trade Association.